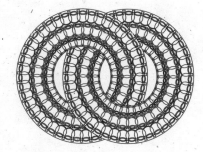

Uncertain Acrobats

Uncertain Acrobats

REBECCA HART OLANDER

CavanKerry Press

PRESS

CavanKerry Press Ltd.
Fort Lee, New Jersey
www.cavankerrypress.org

Publisher's Cataloging-In-Publication Data
(Prepared by The Donohue Group, Inc.)
Names: Olander, Rebecca Hart, author. | Wormser, Baron, writer of supplementary textual content.
Title: Uncertain acrobats / Rebecca Hart Olander ; [foreword by Baron Wormser].
Description: First edition. | Fort Lee, New Jersey : CavanKerry Press, 2021.
Identifiers: ISBN 9781933880884
Subjects: LCSH: Terminally ill—Family relationships—Poetry. | Parents—Death—Psychological aspects—
    Poetry. | Fathers and daughters—Poetry. | Loss (Psychology)—Poetry. | Families—Poetry. | LCGFT: Poetry.
Classification: LCC PS3615.L35 U53 2021 | DDC 811/.6—dc23

Cover artwork © Clique Images/Stocksy United
Cover and interior text design by Ryan Scheife, Mayfly Design
First Edition 2021, Printed in the United States of America

Made possible by funds from the
New Jersey State Council on the Arts, a partner
agency of the National Endowment for the Arts.

In addition, CavanKerry Press gratefully acknowledges generous
emergency support received during the COVID-19 pandemic
from the following funders:

Community of Literary Magazines and Presses

New Jersey Arts and Culture Recovery Fund

New Jersey Council for the Humanities

New Jersey Economic Development Authority

Northern New Jersey Community Foundation

The Poetry Foundation

US Small Business Administration

Also by Rebecca Hart Olander
_____

Dressing the Wounds (2019)

for my father,
Thomas Seymour Hart
1944–2012

O, the dying are such acrobats.
Here you must take a boat from one day to the next,

or clutch the girders of the bridge, hand over hand.
But they are sailing like a pendulum between eternity and evening,

diving, recovering, balancing the air.

—Deborah Digges

Contents

Foreword

The loss figured in this book is a grave one—the death of a much-loved parent. For the adult daughter whom you will meet in these pages, no accurate measurement can be made of that rending. Parents bring their children into the world; there is no getting around that initial miracle. So much is to be celebrated in a loving bond between child and parent, so many days devoted to a common yet remarkable connection, days beautifully elaborated by these poems.

To lose a parent, a father in the case of Rebecca Hart Olander, is to take a great fall. One naturally assumes that beneficence will go on forever. Such is the feeling that accompanies a strong bond between child and parent, and that makes deep sense. Both sides are pleased—what could be better? Among the many charms of this book is how carefully the poet knits together a portrait of her beloved father, Tom, from a daughter's shifting point of view. She explores Tom through the lenses of dependence and independence; interrogates how someone so near can still feel, at times, far; and keeps learning about her father even after his death, realizing how vast he was and remains, observing both how he was beyond her—his own man—and yet how familiar. To lose that familiar love is terrible.

The poems in *Uncertain Acrobats* are up to the daunting task. They present scene after scene, continually refreshing the sense of her father and how important his love for her was. Our age is quick to find fault lines, but as the poet acknowledges in her wonderfully deft poem "College Cathexis" where she tries to summon up a grudge, she ultimately fails. Her love is explicit and thorough, which is to say human and imperfect, central and cockeyed. So we see her father, the man who "made me pose and look as if into the distance / of my important life" and whose heroes included "Thoreau, Hazlitt, Willa / Cather" remembered in his physicality—"your sweaty, sun-worn baseball cap, / your skin browned from being in the world, / early fall 1979, and every beautiful muscle showed / in your legs and your flashing smile." She gives him to us in the fullness of time, right there even as it inevitably recedes.

The poems show us how love doesn't recede, that as we nurture memory we can, through the formative work of imagination, confront the ravages of absence. In acknowledging those ravages, Rebecca Hart Olander is unsparing. Such acknowledgment is part of the respect and devotion due to her dead father. Yet even more prominent—and true and just—is the evocation of his life and her ties to that life, how those ties were strong and original, the gift of this man to that daughter. The poems tell a particular story but they tell a universal one, too, which complements their depth and range. The poet encompasses two lives dramatically and sensitively, lives that were, at once, separate and fused. We can't get away from loss, nor should we want to. These poems reveal our mortal vulnerability as our abiding strength.

Baron Wormser
Montpelier, VT
January 2021

Supermoon

When full and coinciding
with its closest advance on Earth,

light breaks into the living room,
soaking the floor with moon.

Bigger and brighter, this perigee,
washing out the Perseids.

My brother walks toward me
on the deck of a summer party

and—trick of evening light,
flick of what the heart wants—

our father is there.
We look, but we don't see.

Then there's lunar apogee,
the monthly swing away.

They dangle, our gone beloveds,
near as moons.

I.

learning to release

Tickseed

Coreopsis, little yellow explosions,
abundant and obvious as sunshine,
so why the evening nickname, Moonbeam,
misnomer in my book, conjuring bars
of white evening light, outer space,
shallow graves. These are weedy, the greenery
cut out for the side of the road, and hearty,
like little stalks of pine. Mine came from
my grandmother's garden, but not the house
my father grew up in, where St. Francis stood
waiting for wild rabbits and yard birds,
his concrete skirts always empty of crumbs.
She divided these from the strip outside
her later apartment, from after my grandfather died,
and Jason the dog. This, the home of what was
left after the house sold, of favorite things,
and of anything that would grow in a garden
full of stones. Leaves like needles, drought-
tolerant, rabbit-resistant. Give me winter,
you patch of yellow fever, you loosed sachet
of December forest. I cannot cotton your tiny joys
multiplied, creating a cheery thicket year by year,
nor your other name, because your seeds
look like those tiny insects I fear and have
grown vigilant about. How you suck me back
to a time when everything was alive.

Origins

From a place of bird feeders he came,
of glass straws for hummingbirds, of the concrete
feet of St. Francis beneath his robe in the backyard.
From breakfast nook and kitchen pass-through,
serrated grapefruit spoons and maraschino cherries.
From Bakelite and lazy Susan.
Pink sink. Dixie cups. Pixie haircuts.

From a totem pole bought in Banff. From beards,
mustaches, and loafers. 45s, smoking, and tennis.
From Connecticut, the middle of the family chain,
after an uncontainable big sister, but before a soft-spoken
baby brother and the three children who died. He took
the role of peacemaker, their father at the table head,
carving a dead bird every November with pride.

And later, his father bewildered, in a chair
on wheels, rails around the toilet, an adjustable bed.
From cancer he came. He came from a teacher,
his mother's grade book and her lips left
on crushed cigarettes. From hearts, bridge,
and canasta. Crossword puzzles and a den.
TV trays, sectionals, and bronze.

From a childhood where his father made him
and his siblings rewrap their presents after opening
them, so the scene would retain a perfect gleam
through Epiphany. On the shelf under the window,
a little wooden bird with eggs inside her that could
be taken out and played with. In his room, a bag
of marbles. He came from *Treasure Island*.

From slide carousels and Adirondack summers,
lamb and mint jelly under taxidermy and antler racks.
From Tab and birch beer, a cooler like an Airstream
camper. His father dressed as Father Time,
waiting on the porch for his sister's date to bring her
home. He came from college, the same one
as his father before him. From fraternity.

He was Omar Sharif-in-*Doctor Zhivago* handsome.
He came from acoustic guitar, ponytail, and patched
bell-bottoms. From a first marriage to a girl he loved
that lasted just three years. He got off the school bus
he and my mother were riding with friends toward
Colorado, deciding to go instead to divinity school.
They only made Chicago, but he had a vision,

so they hitched back East with dried lentils
and two dollars in pocket. It was 1970.
On my birth certificate the following year,
under Father of Child, he claimed Magician
as Usual Occupation. For Industry or Business,
he is enshrined as a World-Wide Magician
on my government document. By then he was

working a hotline for troubled teens, first stint
as an English teacher and ministerial dreams behind him.
Trays of slides. Ice bucket. Brass fireplace poker.
Encyclopedia volumes. Beefaroni Chess Tournament.
Krishnamurti. Woodstock. I made the mistake
most of us make. I didn't ask enough questions.
When was there time, with all the laughing?

The Mostly Vacant Photo Album of My Parents' Short Marriage

Browned velum cracks

        and separates

    from the spine.

Pages of empty

        white sleeves,

    then a Kodak of my mother

at their wedding reception,

        hair clasped

    in a barrette, cigarette

between her fingers,

        looking fourteen.

    She's nineteen,

nineteen and alone on the page

        with the red tip

    of her Camel.

The back of my dad

        in another shot,

    hiding from posterity.

Before the Divorce

In the lush grass,
my legs positioned into a V,
my back holds the perfect posture
only the new-to-sitting possess.

I am a tripod, two legs and a torso,
wearing a diaper and a seersucker sun hat,
playing with a hose nozzle,
the trickle caught on camera.

I was not yet a year, my parents
twenty-seven and twenty-two in this scrap
of summer, the comedy of small hands
attempting an impossible task.

Maybe they too propped themselves
on the lawn, wearing little, chasing me
when I folded and started to crawl away.
Perhaps it was a picnic, with sandwiches

wrapped in waxed paper. Perhaps
they were newly wed enough
to kiss deeply between bites
of the peaches they'd packed.

Adirondack Paradelle

I perform the summer rituals in my octopus bathing suit.
I perform the summer rituals in my octopus bathing suit.
Wearing six of Grandpa's sun hats at a time, for fun.
Wearing six of Grandpa's sun hats at a time, for fun.
Wearing a suit of hats, I perform for fun, Grandpa's sun.
Bathing in the time, rituals octopus my summer at six.

My head, a tower in terrycloth; I hold apples with my skirt for the deer.
My head, a tower in terrycloth; I hold apples with my skirt for the deer.
Pregnant sounds of coins slivering in the soda machine, and of rain.
Pregnant sounds of coins slivering in the soda machine, and of rain.
I skirt the rain in my terrycloth, hold a tower of coins for soda. My head
pregnant with sounds of deer and apples in the slivering machine.

Grandma waits under clouds on the musty-planked cottage porch.
Grandma waits under clouds on the musty-planked cottage porch.
Near the hummingbird sugar water, in a white tennis outfit and Keds.
Near the hummingbird sugar water, in a white tennis outfit and Keds.
The musty Keds and tennis-white Grandma outfit the cottage. Sugar waits
under water in clouds on a planked porch. Hummingbird, near.

Grandma in clouds of tennis white. Grandpa's outfit, terrycloth. I, water.
The hummingbird with the octopus, bathing in the musty hold of
summer rituals. Pregnant deer perform for my sugar and apples,
I, for coins and soda. At six, wearing a fun suit under my skirt, Keds,
hats in a tower. Near the planked cottage porch, slivering in the sun.
My head, a time machine, waits on sounds of rain.

Ode to Throw Pillows

Lined up along the window seat of the cottage
my grandparents rented in the circle of seasonal
dwellings around Little Moose Lake,

three square pillows: their bony piping
asserting upright shapes the color
of butter, mint leaves, sea glass.

My inheritance, they rest in my guest room,
down flattened and fabric worn, the stain of years
darkening their bright geometry,

survivors from a lost time of grandparents
and summer vacations, curling up
with a can of Tab and a solitaire deck,

or escaping with a book that dropped me
on a seaweed-strewn shore,
or better yet, beneath the waves.

Until Now

The summer of the white deer
we were vigilant. Patiently posed
with palms of peanuts and fruit
on the cedar steps of our community
of cabins. Even my father played
St. Francis. Most of us never saw
the lone doe, slices of McIntosh
and Northern Spy left browning in piles
on porch rails. My hands smelled
of nuts that season, and my pockets
held traces of apples, an orchard after
harvest, before frost steals the scent.
We heard about sightings of her,
from the deepest woods,
where the sun never dappled
the ferns, and once, she ventured
to the overgrown tennis courts,
out by the compound edge, then slipped
behind the caved-in outhouse
like a ghost. Did she know we dreamed
of catching her, our apples a lure?
She stayed in shadows,
where we could not pin down
her hide to a shade of white,
her eyes to a depth of brown,
her nose to a degree of slick.
She was a poem, unwritten.

"Brown Penny"

In a picture from my father's wedding, I loll
on my grandmother's fur coat, hair mingling with pelt.
For the ceremony, I wore a pink-skirted dress
with a white bodice, spray of flowers across the front.

I kept asking when it would be time for cake.
I was seven, already with my own wedding
dreams centered on dresses and desserts.
A Yeats poem was printed in the program—

Go and love, go and love, young man,
If the lady be young and fair. It was 1979, March,
the Year of the Sheep. My dad was thirty-four.
Wasn't he old? Wasn't his new wife old too?

One cannot begin it too soon. But hadn't he
begun love, with my mother, before I was even
born? And though the poem read, *I am looped*
in the loops of her hair, would I remain his girl?

She gave me my first journal,

had me do an exercise

      using all my senses

            to describe a strawberry,

my earliest poem:

      the tiny yellow seeds

            and green hair,

the ripe, misshapen heart,

      the way the red stained

            my fingers in summer,

in my mouth

      the cool exploding

            without sound.

Trigger

Growing up, I watched the tape turn yellow
        on the *New Yorker* cartoon
hung on the fridge, eventually so accustomed
        to the picture
I stopped looking at it. Under ambered strips,
        a man sat up in bed,

clutching his stomach, his wife asleep beside him,
        his eyes shifted to the kitchen,
where an icebox said, *Hmmmmm.*
        The text read, *Ask not*
for whom the refrigerator hums . . .
        it hums for thee.

Do you all remember this too, those of you
        still alive, my brother who once dressed
in capes and crowns, the other not then
        old enough to read, my stepmother
perhaps the one to cut it out and save it
        back in late November, 1980?

Or was it you, gone father, recognizing in yourself
        that wide-awake man,
always craving something in the night, your appetite
        so strong for life and all its delights?
Maybe you chuckled over it
        together, stuck it there

where it became not only image but trigger,
        returning you to that morning of
pie for breakfast after Thanksgiving, oilskin cloth
        printed with black cherries,
pushing the magazine toward the one you love,
        anticipating familiar laughter.

I didn't get, then, the allusion to the tolling bell,
        or how our minds run wild
with all we want, enough to wake us up
        from sleeping. I only knew you knew
something I didn't, and that made me feel young
        and green about the world, which I was.

Lilac Sundays

On weekends, over the years, our family went
to the annual flowering at the Arnold Arboretum,
where panicles of blossoms in mid-May were
at their height, bunches of corollas dripping
from boughs in that sanctuary for trees. We'd spread
our checked cloth and picnic in a cloud of sweetness
and bees. That there could be an arboretum.
That there could be that many different shades of purple.
These outings showed me that, and the names for birds
and their calls as other days we'd walk Mount Auburn
Cemetery with binoculars and quartered peanut-butter-
and-jellies. That a cemetery could be a place for life.
That we could go pioneering through a yard of graves
and see beauty in the markers. That we could scan
branches for flickering feathers, follow a dash of red
or blue across the sky to find where it landed,
waiting there with eyes trained on the greenery until
it flew again. We took out the battered Peterson
and went looking through its pages for what revealed
itself in the air. This taught me patience, to look
around, and to try to name what was singing there.

Joint-Custody Commute

Driving the expressway, my father quizzes me on my times tables while on the oldies station Elvis croons about wise men and fools rushing in. The buildings of Revere and Chelsea fly by, the dump a sloping hill of grass and seagulls, the Tobin Bridge a swooping emerald scaffold for a roller coaster. Dad confidently tosses two quarters into the toll basket, chiming green light bells. Swarms of swallows fill the air and the city comes up like Oz on Dorothy's horizon. I wear the rose-colored glasses that still fit at twelve, turn up the radio when Herman's Hermits sing about Mrs. Brown's lovely daughter. Cracking the triangle of window in the Volkswagen, cranking open the sunroof like a sardine can, I let in the dirty silted river scent rising from the Mystic. It is at once strange and familiar. When we get to Dad's, it will be time for napkins on laps, floss, and homework. For now we are in the no-man's-land of the commute where multiplication is an activity to pass the time, and I can just as easily recite the facts as sing along with the King.

Algebra

He tried to teach me math I didn't want to learn,
hoped I'd stay in Honors, to honor my potential.
Borrowed a book for the upcoming year to study
over the summer, the text already battle worn,
plus it was July, and I was thirteen, on vacation
with no friends except Cyndi Lauper on cassette,
validating that all I really wanted to do was have fun,
that it was what all girls wanted, only that.

I had no idea he couldn't do the equations either,
schooling himself the day before, then explaining it to me
as if he knew what he was doing. I resented it then, thickly,
refusing understanding. How noble his attempts were
seen through time's convex mirror. He didn't have the key,
only the bluster of a father pretending to know how to solve
a problem. Each chapter a puzzle of calculations,
and he held some faith in my ability to do the work.

Anything with numbers and I was a numbskull:
cribbage, cards, chess. Keeping score in the program
at Fenway, shading in the boxes for what meant ball
and what meant strike. What meant error.
He was 68 years on the planet, 41 of which I was his
daughter, unfathomable sums, but some things stuck:
complex roots, subtraction and division
operations, how to carry the zero.

Driving Lessons

I.

In an abandoned school parking lot in Brewster, Massachusetts in August of 1987, my father let me climb in the driver's seat of his white Ford station wagon. Then past cranberry bogs where I couldn't see the fruit but imagined it bobbing there, a million apples waiting to be bitten from their tub. He thought it best to teach me on automatic, let me feel the weight of being in charge of a two-ton hunk of steel before learning to release a clutch or shift gears. He showed me how to switch lanes, to gradually ease from one place to another.

II.

The only driving instructor in Gloucester wore white go-go boots and miniskirts, was about 4'10" and was known to sip liquor from the plaid tin thermos at her feet. A middle-aged Mod girl, belly blown up from vodka and a life of riding in the passenger seat. No wonder she pumped that dual brake so often, stuck looking at youth and all its potential, so ripe she could smell it on us, the sun slathering our dark or strawberry hair, our faces unperturbed till we forgot to blink, and she called us on it.

III.

I dreaded practicing the curve of Cherry Hill Road, the part of the driving test where it's hard to have faith in brakes, its twist the tightest chute in the board game that sends you sliding back a row. One slippery mistake, like the time I pushed my younger brother into the hamper on the landing above the stairs. An exposed nail carved a bloody line down his back, then he ricocheted and tumbled to the bottom. He was howling then, and there was no room for reasons, for the story of how he drove me to it.

IV.

When I took the wheel, it wasn't long after my first period. I called out—half proud, half horrified—to my mother's boyfriend, the only one home, to get me a washcloth to stuff in my pants. After waiting for it for so long, how was I still surprised by that first viscous stain, brownish red as a second-grade papier-mâché volcano? Learning stick is not unlike sex, getting the hang of easing up on the clutch and pressing down on the gas, the balance of power and restraint that makes it possible to be transported, and try not to hurt anyone.

Tidal Basin

That time I stood at the stove in your Dorchester Victorian,
stirring Cream of Wheat, and I was well into high school,
popping the daily pink oval of birth control,
drinking too much Milwaukee's Best on the weekends,
working at the Italian deli back home in Gloucester

where they let me leave with the leftover baguettes
and slabs of Havarti with dill, and too often I got stoned
to the point of paranoia, like that night my friends and I smoked
in the garage of the Museum of Science in Boston before going
to the planetarium where my body forgot how to breathe,

and sometimes if I couldn't decide between turnover or Danish
on the bakery run in the mornings, I'd get both, and I was
vaguely depressed or explicitly so, notching callous boys
on my proverbial belt, learning to navigate drunken donuts
on ice in a borrowed hatchback, always freezing on some dock

chosen for a make-out venue, or by a dying fire in the woods,
or amidst the gravestones of strangers and their kin,
and at the stove, with my back to you, I stirred
the wooden spoon, lost in how the cereal congealed,
and you told me that my butt looked big, in no uncertain terms,

and I was glad my face was turned to the wall,
and I focused on the penguin salt-and-pepper shakers
on the back of the stove, and on the silence
that settled, a thickness in which time expanded,
and I knew I'd never unhear your words.

You must have worried about me, but why couldn't you
have said that? You, who sent me the postcards I still have,
of woodland animals picnicking, sending up bottle rockets,
and going for country drives, addressed to my mother's house
when I was too young to stay with you overnight.

And once I could, family outings on Sundays,
then half the summer, twilight walks looking for rabbits
in the beach rose underbrush, by those eight-inch-high slats
you called bunny fences. You brought me on boats
shaped as swans in Boston's Public Garden,

got me Sports Bars when the vendors walking the steps
between seats at Fenway cried out, *Hey, ice cream here!*
and you made me pose and look as if into the distance
of my important life as I perched on the edge of the stage
of the Elizabethan Theatre at the Folger Library in D.C.

That same trip, we circled the Tidal Basin in a pedal boat
for two under April vacation cherry blossoms. I was fourteen,
my clothes all outfits picked to match. I feel so tender
toward the two of us in that rented vessel, baby brother
and stepmom at the rim, looking on through a storm of petals.

Years later, when you said those words in the kitchen,
did you feel sorry as soon as you did? And what hurt me more,
that you were right, or that you were disappointed in me?
Did you love me a little less because I'd changed?
Did I love you a little less after you said so?

College Cathexis

My girlfriends all seemed to hate their fathers.
       I, too, wanted to burn with righteous fire.
Stoking remnant embers, how mine could have been
       better, I smoldered in my dorm room,
carefully curated with posters of Rosie the Riveter
       and Frida's unapologetic eyebrow,
listening to Liz Phair's *Exile in Guyville* on repeat.

Fathers represented patriarchy and restrictions.
       Chain-link fence. Stuffed shirts. Scarecrows.
Some fathers were active volcanoes, and after eruption,
       their daughters dressed in ashes,
were like Pompeii, held static in their becoming—
       that running girl caught in pyroclastic flows,
that child forever frozen in her small chair.

Thinking of my father that way,
       I fanned my modest disappointments
to try and catch a spark. It didn't take.
       I doused the sputtering flame,
let time transform that old terrain.

My Aesop

It goes like this:

Father Bear was gone. Mother Bear was the one
entering through the swinging door—*Surprise!*—
a blazing cake in her paws.

When he was in the story, he wore a vest
and a very smart hat. He smoked a pipe,
laughed a deep huff of a laugh.

As a cub, I asked him to please hug me more.
Could his distance mean he didn't care,
since Mother Bear cradled me close in our den?

Little Ursula, I wore my heart on my fur.
Once a yearling newly on my own,
I circled the familiar territory of that wound,

as if he hadn't offered a remedy.
But that wasn't the lesson.
When I asked, he answered,

pride set aside, the ways of his kind.
He wrapped his shaggy arms around me
and held on.

Peine forte et dure

I remember getting stoned with my father
in the backyard of his house in Boston.
All lightness and insight. Intoxicating.
Summer night, a creeping darkness,
both struck dumb by the sound
of crickets singing rounds
with passing cars in the gathering dusk.

When his final darkness came,
he didn't want to look, but in life,
he'd walked through Concord as bold
and sure as Thoreau, stacking cairns
he hoped fellow travelers
would add to, finding comfort
in revisiting, and in change.

In elementary school, a field trip
to the Salem Witch Museum, where a waxen
Giles Corey died slowly beneath heavy stones
over and over in his cell, his strained voice
answering only: *More weight.*
On Corey's memorial marker:
Pressed to Death, September 19, 1692.

A pretty name for it, *peine forte et dure,*
punishment for those refusing to plead.
In a way, my father "stood mute,"
unable to speak at the end. I'd like to think
he was riding high on the scent
of long-ago Rose of Sharon trees
in the city, the chorus of cicadas.

Josephine Grace

A lobe of lung the plan, but he took it all, that German surgeon, who told us
afterward that it had gone well, but that of course you'd never run again.

That was January, 2009. From your hospital bed, we watched
Obama's first inauguration, hope seeping into the room.

Then rehab on the small track of living room to kitchen,
then into the meadows with the loons and herons, eventually

a marathon-long walk, a mile-long run, so you proved him wrong.
Then four years laced with travels, Tarceva, and gratitude.

When the cancer returned, it took you in seven weeks. December, 2012,
we saw Sandy Hook unfold on the news in your room at Mass General.

We buried you in the back of a cemetery named for a saint,
your only neighbor in that expanse a little girl from Newtown,

whose family moved north after the shooting. She was autistic
and could never speak, putting your lost voice into perspective.

She turned seven three days before she was killed, and you'd turned sixty-eight
a few days before that. She helped me be glad for the length of your life.

II.

no trampoline

Find Alternate Routes

is what the digital road sign flashed
at me as I drove downtown,
as if there is another path through this thicket,
as if we are sleeping beauties
and can be kissed out of our darkness,
as if we can cut away kudzu
and it will stop letting down its insidious hair,
as if we can uproot bittersweet
and it will cease its blood red choking of the lilacs,
as if you will be unchanged,
robust like you were when I was seven
and we crouched together in mirrored pose
mimicking the stance of breaking into a run,
me in my burnt orange corduroy jumpsuit,
hair parted to the side and clasped with a barrette,
my blue Keds beside your running sneakers
still laced tight from the hometown 5K you raced
in your sweaty, sun-worn baseball cap,
your skin browned from being in the world,
early fall 1979, and every beautiful muscle showed
in your legs and your flashing smile,
oh, damn this route you are racing now,
all those other games gone,
your detour paved with brittle prognosis,
coasting swells nothing like the adrenaline
that used to course through,
making you feel every inch a man.

The Cancer Is Back

We blend bone meal with soil at the base of rosebushes,
tendering roots with the dust of other lives.
It is this life I want, we seem to say,
with each swath of dead perennials we clear,
making way for what we assume will come.
But there is nothing to mix into this unspeakable void.
The cells are doing their dire multiplying,
and we already fed them all our best poison.
Can you stand to enter those changing rooms again?
The metallic pull across of the striped curtain,
the flimsy wraparound of a backwards robe?
Couldn't you go on seeking cyber chess domination,
tying up pork loins stuffed with apricots and sage,
wearing the vest you bought in Santa Fe
until the buttons all fall off?
No more pinpoint tattoos!
Your single lung has only just learned to live alone.

Veterans Day on Authors Ridge

Sun slips between coniferous branches,
       and under bronzy switches of fallen

pine, the bones of Alcott, Thoreau,
       expired Ebenezers and Elizas.

Flags flicker atop mausoleums and along
       the winding paths,

brotherhood planes fly their noisy formations,
       and the neighbor across the street

rakes his leaves. I envy the task,
       the way what he piles will compost

into something smaller, how he can sort
       what has come undone.

There's No Place Like Home

Finding the screech owl holed up below the canopy
of the spindle tree, auburn feather fist in austere bark,
my father suggests we turn back for binoculars.

I had never seen a daylight owl,
only heard the dusky cries, feeling as mice
must, quivering in a field beneath wing-blotted stars.

Through doubled glass we focus on the russet
bird, casting her as an avian wizard behind the curtain.
But some things can't be known until we know them.

Like what kind of call we will make
as the predator descends, digs in her talons,
and shakes us until we are still.

Circling Great Meadows

Over muddied paths rimed with ice,
hard black stars of water chestnut pods,
ornaments of invasion,
smother the marsh with their dark beauty.
At a small bridge over a diminished stream,
we cross the worn slats
and feel the wood bend beneath us,
supple compared to the hardening ground.

Surfaces dismay. Unknowable country,
unknowable me, unknowable you.
Our story is mapped in tree bark,
but when it peels away, what will be left?
For now, the heart still beats
beside the steadfast lung untwinned,
a body unmanned, unmoored, untethered,
unabashed at all its wanting.

A raft of ducks moons our passing,
rear feathers pointing toward diluted wintry sky,
bills full of water and weeds.
How many mouths gasped then,
for final breaths, for first breaths?
And what is the difference
between a question with no answer
and a question never asked?

Turritopsis dohrnii

In a tenth-floor hospital room, my father survives surgery
with scars, the tang of residual fear, and green Jell-O.
The besieged brain chugs along, the scalp peeled open,
shunt placed, cancer given marching orders to the abdomen.

My stepmother leans in, and he jokes, *Do you want to have sex?*
He with half a head of hair, glued together like Mary Shelley's
nightmare, we three children attendant in the room.

Uncertain acrobats, we tightrope between existing and
living, the patient with a new cane and an incomplete grasp
of gravity, the rest of us sinking under too much of it,
jealous of his morphine, of the wishful thinking he floats in.

At the bedside, my brother reads aloud how some jellyfish
are immortal, the medusa transforming: first the deterioration
of the bell, then the tentacles, cells transdifferentiating,

bypassing death. But who would want to suffer constant
regeneration? The wounded head, the dark internal drip
of cells. When should be the end of such continuing?

Grand Central Station

The information kiosk is his brain, the hub of necessary info,
but the lines are long, and sometimes the clerk has no answers.

The vaulted teal ceiling with its gods in star patterns: heaven.
The golden box in the wall for sending letters: his bulletin board,

which we collage with his devoted, unread fan mail.
The trains arriving, departing: a battery of drugs traveling his veins

to try to kill the cancer, stop the nausea, repress the seizures,
kindle the appetite, loosen the bowels, ease the pain.

Track lines: unwanted tattoos along his weary arms,
the conditions pushing back, winning the war, always clearly

winning the war, no matter the little battles won. He is still
as the marble floors and steps of the terminal. He is terminal,

the gray-white shade of statues, and we are the tourists—
doctors, nurses, aids, hospice, therapists, sons, daughter, wife,

friends, clergy, palliative team—all of us looking to the ceiling
for answers, bustling around pretending we know where we are

going. Below, the sewers churn with packs of rats, the gods above
keep their fixed positions, and our every action glances off stone.

Glossolalia

Pulling into the parking garage requires steeling
yourself before getting out, before going in
through the revolving doors, before entering the elevator
that stops at the unholy neurology floor
where patients speak in tongues and sometimes know it,
partial loss pushing them to the edge of a skyscraper
they hold onto with only fingernails,
sure they will fall, and that there will be no trampoline,
and maybe they think of deities
with arms waiting to hold them in the hereafter,
but it won't feel like wives feel, like daughters.
It won't even feel as abrasive as nurses
when they gather the body like a bundle of sticks
and roll it over and again to strip the soiled linens.

Husk

This is what is left
when language leaves
us—the humming,
the seesaw breath
in and out,
and images of
who my father was:
long-distance runner,
cross-country coach,
English teacher, essayist,
rabid reader, belter of song
and strummer of chords,
backgammon partner,
the last one up at night
reading under dim light,
his strong tea, loose,
from Ireland,
his measuring the leaves,
his steeping overlong,
cream in the stained
vessel, the dark well,
a ritual leading
his inner lion
to the easy chair,
to make that lion
lie down with the lamb
he kept looking for.

Advent Calendar

Each morning, Max slips his finger under the flap,
revealing the image for the day:
bells, cherubic angels, a wreath of pine.

Nothing thrills now, this torn month
a blur of tears, tubes, and hospital trays.
This season is not wanting for surprise.

Perhaps someday a wooden train, pig-tailed doll,
or Bethlehem's star will seem a gift.
Feigning interest in camouflaged gates and windows,

we pretend to care what today will bring.
Batten the hatches, bar the doors!
Let's not daily reopen this December.

Red Cloud

I swallowed the dye, crushed pills, applesauce.
I thanked the angel who changes the sheets
and knocks before entering. When she shaved me,
everyone thought I was unaware, but I knew the smell,
the lather, the brisk blade scratching along my throat.
I breached then, in my black pond, perked to her
touch, a warm towel afterward, tingling pores.

Sons debate bacon on pizza, daughter's pen scratches
paper, noting my care. And wife weeps in my ear,
whispering her love. TV hums in the corner, but I'm done
with Patriots now, with Rondo's missed three-pointers.
My runner's heart keeps time, but my heart isn't in it.

Drugs help. And Paul Simon. Matchbook, smoky ski lodge,
circle of stuffed wolves. Old camp song about creatures
in God's choir, me the badger gray and full of sighs,
talking to myself like the porcupine. Flickering reels,
tenth birthday bike, sister Hilary's dark eyes, Yaz-signed ball.
The thread, what is the thread . . . I am not who I was,
last week office organizing, phoning Bebe singing birthday . . .

Unable to say, *Remember Santa Fe?* Adobe apartment
we dropped our bags and stayed. Sun hats and heaps
of oranges and all the time ahead of us. She rubs my hand,
my face, as if to tug me up, pull me back to air, to light,
make me say *my dove,* say the grave won't stop my care.

But I pray: *Zeus! Hurl your lightning at my heart.*
Make a crater I can topple into. Summer ruler, storm king,
bolt me with your wonder remedy, your fatal shaft.
Dear ones, when you see those bleached bone skulls,
you'll have me, and when you turn Cather's pages, you'll find
me in Red Cloud, the simple house, wide yellow seas outside,
split-rail fence, and the little graveyard's faded, sloping stones.

Fortune

The grim was in the sky this morning,
etched in smokestack breath,
black dog of death in profile,
gaping mouth, doubled ridge of teeth,
smudged at the edges, foretelling today's end.

We think you'll die by nightfall;
the palliative team made its gentle proclamation.
There isn't much left of you: hollow in your middle,
concave chest where they carved out one lung,
hair falling out across your pillow.

Yet there is everything:
hands to hold that are warm, closed eyes
suggesting the way you napped through summer storms
and on winter afternoons after wading in gaiters
through the snow behind your house.

Now that we have held you under
and you still know how to breathe,
I know you are the god I thought you were,
and that your god is just a tricky monkey,
peeling away your layers.

Squatting in the corner of the room,
he juggles with the hours you have left,
makes your hands swell and recede,
chills the soles of your feet,
and causes you to seize and vomit blood.

Morphine, Dilantin, Valium, Keppra,
the one that dries your mouth and keeps you
from choking on your own sustenance.
How are we standing for these standing orders?
How are you lying down?

Ascension

At the base
of the mountain,
in a hollow filled
with flowers never
seen, the burro waits
with your bags strapped
on his sloping back,
a shawl of sun drapes
your shoulders, a finished
book by your side,
a packed pipe, a full
wineskin, soft leather
boots laced tightly
for the climb,
and in the distance,
your dreams still
catching up with you,
raising dust clouds
as they go, the scent of
lemons and cinnamon,
curl of coffee rising
from a cup, rainclouds
holding steady
in a sky about to
unlock, the future
delighting itself
without you.

III.

riding the wind

Fool's Gold

You fly at me, lurching memory, trapeze
artist, my pendulum. This swing dance, a trap,
the way summer slips into fall with ease.

Sometimes it hurts too much. It's a shallow
river, and I'm panning for pyrite. Walking, I allow
myself to imagine you there, under branches slung low.

On every hike, I anticipate you at the top of the mountain,
pain a packhorse I learn, foot in the stirrup, then the mount,
grasping saddle horn like a novice, counting slowly to ten

before pulling back gently on the reins. This triangle:
you, me, and the mottle-winged messenger with the angle
that sorrow can't be shunned, a swooping, scavenger gull

leaking cries as steam hisses from a broken radiator.
In your icy absence, the sun keeps trying to radiate.
There's no forgetting. Something was dislodged, and tore.

Feeding the Dead

What is it that eats us alive? So hungry for us
that it leaves holes in the world afterward?

Like the angel's share of whiskey from the barrel,
disappeared not into oak but ether, the mouths of spirits.

Is it the ancestors, populating the greenery
as twittering birds, rustling the leaves?

The way the hermit thrush isn't there, then is,
or spider's thread, suddenly silver in the morning

when you step to one side. I wanted my father to stay,
but maybe his mother was more ravenous.

Visitation

In the folds of old flannel
draped over my closet door,
my father's face manifest, wizened
in profile, knob-nosed and knowing,
a Germanic folktale illustration.

When I look close, he's disappeared
back into the underbrush,
unblinking eyes watching me
from so deep in bracken, I can only catch
the slightest scent on sleeves.

I grasp for more,
but it is crumbs left in the wood,
glinting in moonlight,
illuminating the way,
no matter how hard I try to get lost.

The Highway

Aphasia. None of us knew what to say. Malignancy mapped in the coils of your
Brain, the gathered words of your heroes under attack: Thoreau, Hazlitt, Willa
Cather. Cancer cells coursed up and down the route of your spine,
Diagnosis grim, seven weeks all it took, though we cut and shaved and medicated,
Eradicating who you were to try to keep you here a little longer.
Forgetting: more of it happens each day. But I still remember the
Glossolalia, language tossed like a salad, the words all out of their places.
How tightly you held my hand when you couldn't speak at all.
I stood beside you, tethering your fear, while under your cot a circling
Jackal laughed, waiting for the inevitable.
Kindness. Was it risking seizure, just to see your open eyes, or holding you under?
Lyrics about liberation and release from a Crowded House song.
My dear one, your dying was the deepest splinter, amputation, dead bell, downed
Nest. I don't know what to think about souls.
Outside your hospital window, the golden dome of the State House, gas lamps ran
Parallel, all the way up and down Beacon Street. It's not as if you
Quit. Shaking, your eyes rolled into your head, and you foamed, like a
Rabid dog. We put you down, telling ourselves it was mercy.
So what now? Writing about your death is a way to avoid writing about your life,
Things I know a finite set, and fading by the day. A bear-shaped
Umbrella stand, carved arms held like a ballerina in first position.
Valentine paradelle you wrote for your wife. That you broke a five-minute mile.
Wild are the moors of what I don't know and now can never ask.
Xylem, your well-worn Scrabble word, you at the end, your body straining,
Your brain wandering in fields of heather, half ghost. In the end, we were all
Zombies, speechless, holding our arms out, nothing resting there.

Easter, after You've Gone

This year, no one has the fortitude to place the familiar figures on the table. Little Bo Peep, her rusted bell. The bunnies and the gnomes. Goldilocks with her frayed braids and her three bears. Girl in the red felt cape. The wolf. They are nesting in their box in the dark.

You aren't here to tuck garlic cloves and rosemary into the secret folds of butterflied lamb. You're the shepherd boy sleeping by the haystack, so soundly you don't know what you're missing. We're toasting you, Dad, with the good Montepulciano. Bunches of grape hyacinth fill the air with bruised longing.

We walk around the marsh after dinner, find a three-trunked tree teaming with newborn ladybugs massing in the crotches as if the bark were bleeding, a slow and steady drip released from wooden seams. Geese own the walks, their curved necks threatening, shepherd's crooks poised to herd us into the abyss.

Mockingbird Elegy

We trekked the Chesterfield Gorge, alongside the Westfield River,
        that vast watershed that drains from twenty-nine towns
        to join the Connecticut, emptying into the Atlantic.
We did not see the yellow bellies and tufted crowns of cedar waxwings,
        nor their rakish batgirl masks, black smears across their eyes,
        brilliant red wax droplets on their wingtips.
They did not leave their leafy forest homes to meet us
        on the path, nor did they converge in aerial clashes
        over rushing water in pursuit of mayflies.
We did not glimpse translucent jelly tooth mushrooms
        mimicking the tails of white whales cresting
        above the ocean's surface, undersides tined as mouths.
When glancing up into the mossy forest opposite the gorge,
        we did not see stone walls and cellar holes among the ash,
        beech, and maple, no remnants of human history.
We did not see the Riffle Snaketail dragonflies,
        who begin their lives underwater before becoming
        flashes of color in the air above the river.
From their riparian and wet deciduous habitats, yellow warblers,
        those migratory songbirds, may have called out,
        but they did not leave their cover.
We did make two cairns and thought of you, placing them
        where the rocks had been roller-coastered over time, swollen
        stones shot through with every shade of gray.
You would have loved the eddies where the rocks glistened red beneath
        the surge, and you would have known the birdsongs, each to each,
        mocking the warbler till she was sure you were her beloved.

Calling Song

Walking accompanied by the soundtrack of summer's end:
single leaf falling, squirrels in the underbrush, unseen
as they blend with the gray of last year's leaves,
and the thrum of insects in the greenery,
bushes shimmering with sound, a trilling
that isn't cricket, peeper, or bird.

Back home, my search-bar questions find articles of answers:
"The Sound of August: Jar Fly? Cicada? or Locust?"
and "What Bug's Creating All That Late Summer Buzz?"
The buzz, it seems, is the annual cicada hatching,
the *Tibicen lyricen* calling song,
every year new and alive in its short living.

His old voice is still on the machine:
Hi there, Becky, Dad here. Then the birthday song,
curling out the *to you* in vibrato to make it last longer,
and it does last, but of course it's also gone.

Mourning Walk

The yellow farmhouse down by the playing fields
is for sale. I consider all the cows that have lived there,
making milk and manure. Across the way, the overgrown
and near frozen community garden, and all I can think of
is the gone. It's autumn again, and I am again surprised
at the familiar turning. Fallen crabapple on the sidewalk,
ridden with wormholes, cradled in a half-red leaf.
I talk to my dead father while I walk. A circling hawk
stands in for him, then a flash of cardinal over a field
of dry grasses. Males are brighter birds. That's how he was,
but he made me feel my own brilliance. A scatter of blackbirds
crosses the sky over the road, pepper thrown into soup.
It tangs and tosses. It's fennel in my mouth, and longing.

Remains

                    Wound of winter remains,
yard swath full of ice and rain,
jays fat in the coniferous bush.
                    Woodpecker-pocked trunks.
Red-husked Chinese lantern.
A seesaw, beauty and pain.
                    My father's clothes
still hang in the cedar closet,
stink of unneeded mothballs.
                    The deep freeze kills
the deer ticks, and if bagged
and brought outside overnight,
                    the dust mites multiplying
inside my allergic son's
pillow, his stuffed lion.
                    A thick white grub
shifts quietly in the dark,
a comma in the universal
                    sentence, a pause
before the squash of spring spade.

Without You, I'm an Out-of-Work Engineer

My train of thought barrels down in runaway speed, an old locomotive I thought was rusting through at the salvage yard but haunts me, a heavy shadow. I put on the worn pinstriped hat and look for you, my hobo, my impossible.

I want to follow you down the hill, pell mell like in the Little Golden Book, try to dig in under the fence and still get a helping of something sweet, ever disobedient, loyal and lonely, not wanting to face the consequences.

Recipe for you: Summer camp canvas tents, bury to the neck in sand, call out *Boxcars!* when rolling double sixes in Yahtzee, Fenway franks and Cracker Jacks, Dr. Gravity's Kite Shop, Ovaltine, log your miles run, begin at Heartbreak Hill, play chess by postcard with an old friend, Aesop's fables, Christmas Revels, Elvis Costello and Steely Dan LPs, bowties, your self-taught saxophone, your blue ukulele, unstrung.

My salt runs away with itself, memories jangle, an armful of bangles, a bushel of apples loosed and knocking down the stairs, bruised flesh, and I cannot gather my skirts around this bundle of twigs, matches all soaked through.

Your passing pierced me, subtle knife of frigid knowing, immutable as steel. Memory's suitcase swells with letters of diminishing graphite and ink, book bindings that disintegrate as I navigate, searching for your hand in the margins.

My Father's Burial Clothes

If I could redress you, I'd place jade stones
over your eyes and mouth, string chips of jade
with copper thread to make armor you could wear
into eternity: slippers, leggings, sleeves, gloves, a mask,
a wedge to elevate your head. On the chest piece,
I'd fashion a phoenix lifting above your one good lung.

Then I could picture you as oxidized treasure,
preserved, not getting smaller and smaller
in your best black suit, the pennies we placed
on your coffin too little to pay for the ferry.
Instead, sheathed and shepherded
to another shore by dragon tears.

The Whale

Mine died when I hit middle age, he still young
at sixty-eight. I'll never say we're through.

He is that creature under the cold Atlantic blanket,
migratory mammal, singing a complex song,

large heart beating in time with mine, wide cetacean
smile, throat pleats, fluke, and fin. All that potential

lamplight and winter warmth stored in his immortal bulk.
No harvested baleen, no corset bone. He'll never stop

his route, though sometimes he needs to breach,
and once I dreamed he beached. I tried to drag him back

to the surf, where the salt could lick his wounds
and he could open one eye to the sun.

But that was a nightmare. The truth is in the Gulf
Stream, dark shadow spouting, swimming with seals.

My Heaven Would Be Studded with Fathers

My father in his blue
and white striped bathing suit,
holding me by the ankles,
my hair sweeping
the Good Harbor sand,

my father tossing quarters
into the toll basket as we
cross the Tobin Bridge
toward his house
for the weekend,

my father quizzing me
on the singers
of Motown radio tunes
while we drive, and
on my times tables,

my father stuffed
into a student desk
on Parent Night,
defending my efforts
to my algebra teacher,

my father inhaling
a joint, then passing it
my way on the back steps
of a fading purple
Victorian in Dorchester,

my father in a fisherman's
sweater holding
my swaddled firstborn
with a look on his face
I'd never seen,

my father reading her
Frog and Toad and looking
like Frog or Toad himself,
in his tweed jacket with
patches on the elbows,

my father reading a prayer
to me and my beloved
at our wedding, wearing
seersucker, happy to
bring God into the room,

my father, rendered speechless,
on a gurney, clutching my hand,
in an anonymous corner
at Mass General that I won't
forget the whiteness of,

my father in the woods,
placing stones on top of
other stones, then back
in the woods to see
who's added to his cairns,

then not in the woods at all,
then in the woods everywhere,
my father, in the woods
like stars in the ether, spangling
everything in a wash of light.

The Acolyte at My Door Asks Me, How Do You Pray?

It's always too late, and when I am afraid. I never remember
to prune before the frost or to thank heaven for small favors,
though I didn't forget to stitch the way my father cared for me
into the fabric of how I understand love. A person can die
of not being regarded, inside, in the important places.
If the inverse is true, am I immortal? Is he? Should we wish
to be? Around the house, relentless lilies of the valley,
which I sought, planted, and tended, but they bit back
in spades. Do I even want this return of happiness?

Years now, since my father left me in the snow.
His eyes were closed, and he had already said his last words
weeks before. He was on a path through bittersweet and myrrh,
kudzu and herringbone. I want to say I understand the mysterious
ways in which God moves, but I am unmoved by mystery.
Father, now days go by when I don't think of you. I'm making
a life without, all the clocks ticking the same songs as when
you were alive. How does the world sound the same,
run by its consistent engines, though everything has changed?

Return to Great Meadows

At the gaping center of the marsh, dozers   unearth the earth, upbraid invasive
purple loosestrife. With choking stalks,   these bog sirens trick the terrain
with false beauty. Canada geese honk   in tandem with low-flying planes

from Hanscom Airforce Base. In the distance,   a solitary loon.
Closer, a scurry of chipmunks inhabits the reeds.   The hollow a screech owl
once filled. Dragonflies attached end-to-end,   pinwheels riding the wind.

Scattered stones under cattails, old cairns   undone. Along the watchtower,
silver corners strung with the projects   of spiders. A single cardinal
frets between two trees. Ruddy bird,   flying heart-in-the-bush,

the hue of a berry stain on yesterday's   apron, monthly blood seeped
into a mattress, dusky burn of forsythia   at the brink of fall, rusty
bloom of feminine plumage, mateless   without her scarlet twin.

Is she looking for him? Does the wind tell   her where the owl has gone,
how long the geese will clog the rushes,   how fast this winter will roll in?
What can she tell us, who treat these   meadows like a labyrinth?

Or is the lesson in the bird register,   chalked in the script of many hands,
noting green heron, nuthatches,   and a redwing? What are we
meant to learn from the broken   rosary hanging on the welcome map,

from the found feather, from the way   the binocular case snaps shut
with worn-in ease, from the backs   of benches bearing names of the dead,
or from Peterson's dog-eared pages,   penciled with proof of life?

Do we mostly want to know we have not   been left? Pocketing the heart-
shaped stones pried from where they settled,   we dig incremental graves.
With each removal, in the taking of evidence,   a soothing sort of theft.

Notes

"Trigger": The cartoon referenced was created by Jack Ziegler.

"My Father's Burial Clothes": This poem is inspired by a Chinese jade burial suit from the Han Dynasty (206 BCE–220 CE), which was part of an exhibit entitled "Ancient Treasures" installed at the George Walter Vincent Smith Art Museum in Springfield, Massachusetts from July 2006 to February 2014. This artifact was on display for public viewing for the first time in 2,200 years; I visited in November of 2013, the month before the first anniversary of my father's death.

Acknowledgments

Grateful acknowledgment is given to the editors of the following publications, in which poems in this book have been previously published or are forthcoming, sometimes in different form:

Bracken Magazine: "Visitation"
Lemon Hound: "Return to Great Meadows"
Literary Mama: "Find Alternate Routes"
Plath Poetry Project: "Trigger"
Silkworm: "The Cancer Is Back," "Mockingbird Elegy"
SWIMM Every Day: "The Whale"
30 Poems in November! anthologies: "Before the Divorce," "Veterans Day on
    Authors Ridge"
Waves: A Confluence of Women's Voices anthology: "There's No Place Like Home"
Woven Tale Press: "Grand Central Station," "Supermoon," *"Turritopsis dohrnii"*

Deep appreciation goes to the team at CavanKerry for accepting my manuscript and shepherding it to publication and beyond. Publisher Joan Cusack Handler and Managing Editor Gabriel Cleveland made suggestions that utterly changed the book's shape, making for a stronger, more relatable collection. Content Editor Baron Wormser saw the love and respect in these poems, which made me feel seen in turn. Thank you, Baron, for crafting the generous foreword as well. Copyeditor Joy Arbor's pruning was capable and wise and provided many little epiphanies (and one Epiphany). Thanks to Ryan Scheife of Mayfly Design, Marketing and Communications Director Dimitri Reyes, and Social Media Coordinator Elena Neoh for having my back and that of my book (and its front and interior) as this collection makes its way into the hands of readers. And I'm honored to be in community with such stellar fellow CKP writers.

   I am so grateful to my writing communities for their support through the years of my developing as a poet, losing and missing my dad, and encouraging the writing of what would become this book. A deep bow goes to my two long-term writing groups, whose members include Jean Blakeman, Libby Maxey, Adin Thayer, Sharon Tracey, S. G. Tyler, and Abigail Warren. I'm grateful as well for the Poetry Cleanse folks, where ten of these poems took their first steps.

I'm blessed to be a part of the Vermont College of Fine Arts MFA community. I applied there the fall my dad's cancer returned; the last piece of writing of mine my dad read was my application essay. Thank you to the faculty with whom I was lucky enough to work, especially my advisors Jody Gladding, Tomás Q. Morín, Natasha Sajé, and Betsy Sholl, and to my classmates, particularly Mary Lannon and Elizabeth Paul, who read these poems during a retreat at VCFA in 2019 as I revised it for CavanKerry, and Susan O'Neill.

During another retreat to my hometown of Gloucester, writing friends KT Landon, Kali Lightfoot, Jennifer Martelli, and Carla Panciera provided valuable insights as I was polishing this collection. I'm grateful for editing time afforded through a residency at Patchwork Farms funded by Straw Dog Writers Guild in the summer of 2019 as well. And appreciation goes to Bettina Judd for reviewing a version of this manuscript and helping me to accept permission for telling my experiences my way. This would not be a book without you, each and all.

My group of friends and family is generous in size and heart. Thank you to each of you for loving me through loss, for reading my work, and for sharing this life with me. Without my family of origin, I wouldn't have these experiences to write about—to linger over and mourn and celebrate—and they are not just mine but theirs as well. I can't name each person in this small space, but a few require special recognition.

In memory of my aunt, Hilary Hart, my dad's amazing sister, who was dealt her own cancer card in 2020: right till the end of her life in 2021, she was asking after this book and celebrating my success. Hilary was the consummate keeper and teller of family stories, and I wish she could have held this one. My uncles—my dad's brother Rick Hart and his husband, David Chura—helped me define steadfast love. Rick is also a family history torchbearer, and David shares this writing life and the experience of telling collective yet personal stories and is also one of the biggest champions of my work.

So much love to my brother Peter Hart, who knows more deeply than I what it is to not have a father around, and to my mother, Marcia Hart, for choosing my dad and having me and teaching me by example how to be an advocate and caregiver. To my stepmother, Christopher Jane Corkery, my brothers Patrick and Eamonn Hart, and their beloveds Scott and Megan: these hospital days and after days are ones I shared most intimately with you. Thank you for helping me to find my footing. Patrick and Eamonn, it is a balm to see our dad in you, both physically and in the ways you embody his spirit. And what a gift it was to welcome Eamonn and Megan's son, Thomas Waterman Hart, to the world in 2020. Christopher, your loss, and your own poetic renderings of that, are staggering. Thank you for the love and life you built with my dad, for your poems, and for your love and support of me as I share my own.

Finally, to my circle, my home: Jonathan Olander, you make a pretty terrific dad yourself. I'm glad mine was so dear to you as well. To our children, Monica Hunter-Hart and Maxwell Olander, I will never forget that December of 2012 when you sent me dance videos at the hospital and decorated the house without me, for me. Your Grandpa Tom is part of you. You each keep the light on in my heart, and I love you.

CavanKerry's Mission

A not-for-profit literary press serving art and community, CavanKerry is committed to expanding the reach of poetry and other fine literature to a general readership by publishing works that explore the emotional and psychological landscapes of everyday life, and to bringing that art to the underserved where they live, work, and receive services.

Other Books in the Emerging Voices Series

Uncertain Acrobats has been set in Macklin Sans Light, a sharp yet elegant sans serif font inspired by the era when type leapt off the pages of books and onto large-scale posters and advertisements. It was designed by Malou Verlomme of Monotype.

This book was printed on paper from responsible sources.